Come,
Healing
God

Robert —
This book is
for you —
Blessings,
Barbara B

Come, Healing God

Prayers During Illness

Joan Guntzelman and Lou Guntzelman

Liguori

LIGUORI, MISSOURI

Imprimi Potest:
Richard Thibodeau, C.Ss.R.
Provincial, Denver Province
The Redemptorists

Published by Liguori Publications
Liguori, Missouri
www.liguori.org

A previous edition of this book was published by Saint Mary's Press, Winona, MN 55987.

Library of Congress Cataloging-in-Publication Data

Guntzelman, Joan.
    Come, healing God : prayers during illness / Joan Guntzelman and Lou Guntzelman.—Rev. ed.
        p.   cm.
ISBN 0-7648-1214-9
    1. Sick—Prayer-books and devotions—English. 2. Catholic Church—Prayer-books and devotions—English. I. Guntzelman. Lou. II. Title.

BX2373.S5G86 2004
242'4—dc22   2004057817

The editor and publisher gratefully acknowledge permission to reprint/reproduce copyrighted works granted by the publishers/sources listed on page 113.

Printed in the United States of America
08 07 06 05 04   5 4 3 2 1
Revised edition 2004

To our brother and sisters:
Ray, Mary Ellen, and Carol

Contents

Preface

A traditional saying suggests that prayer is a "lifting of the mind and heart to God." Nothing seems to provoke such an intensive turning to God as do illness, injury, and threats to our well-being. No human being escapes life's assaults or reversals for any length of time. But these times of reversal can be powerful wake-up calls, offering new opportunities to examine the realities and priorities of our life and new moments to learn meaningful prayer—prayer with an original freshness, coming from unsuspected depths.

Though much of our experience may be with formal prayers, the prayers in this book suggest ways to expand our methods of raising our heart and mind to God during crucial times. Along with older, traditional prayers that can give us great comfort, we may be called to discover other ways of praying, reflecting, and gaining understanding of our life with God, in whom "we live and move and have our being" (Acts 17:28). God has promised to be with us in sickness and in health.

USING THE PRAYERS

The intent of this book is to offer suggestions for praying when you are lost for words, overwhelmed with discomfort, fearing treatments, struggling for reasons, searching for meaning, or desiring to know that God is close.

In using this book, find the prayers that best describe your present condition. From the variety of prayers offered, select the one or two that speak to your present distress. Pray the prayer that you need, and come back to it in an hour or a day and let it speak to you again, befriending you, touching your heart like a faithful friend—hour by hour, day by day, week by week, throughout your illness.

As you progress toward health, toward a new stage of life, or toward life after life, you may wend your way through this book, letting the variety of prayers accompany you through your changing moods, emotions, and thoughts. During your journey, seek the God who is with you always, and lift your mind and heart a little or a lot according to the strength given you each day.

SPECIFIC SUGGESTIONS

As you begin your prayer, be attentive to the space you are in: the room and its surroundings, where you are sitting or lying, the pains or comforts of your body, the anxieties or tranquillity of your soul. Invite the Spirit of God to be with you, right here, right now.

Read each prayer slowly and meditatively. Let it speak to you. Savor any line or word that resonates with you. Repeat it. Hold it in your heart. If you choose, read the prayer again, letting its thoughts be your thoughts, its cries be your cries, its voice be your voice. Pause and let the Spirit of God speak to you, bringing you rest or challenge, continuing the gentle but heartfelt dialogue between the two of you.

The prayer reflections on these pages may provide material for further consideration or engagement. You may want to do some journal writing about the thoughts, questions, and feelings that emerge in your prayer. You may want to write your own prayer or your own letter to God. Your prayer may urge you to share with a family member, a friend, a chaplain, or a confidant the concerns and the movements of grace that are coming to you in this time of illness and reversal.

The Gospel invites us "to pray always and not to lose heart" (Luke 18:1). Times of illness, injury, and reversal in life can become privileged moments of knowing and trusting God's enduring love for us, a love that is eternal and infinite.

Prayers
During Illness

God hear my prayer;
let my cry for help come to you.
Since I am in trouble,
do not conceal your face from me.
Turn and listen to me.
When I call, respond to me quickly.

PSALM 102:1–2
Psalms Anew

—◄o►—

What would you say to me, my God,
    after such a plea?…

✝ *"My ears and my heart heard your prayer*
    even before you put it into words.
I'm closer to you than you dream.
You and I will deal with your troubles
    together.
        Count on me."

If we live as we breathe, take in and let go, we cannot go wrong.

CLARISSA PINKOLA ESTÉS
Women Who Run With the Wolves

—◀o▶—

O God of my comings and goings,
you who are with me
in every circumstance of my life,
help me to simply accept what is.

In every condition of my being,
you are here.

When I feel well and am at peace,
may I find my rest in you.

When I suffer and am in distress,
may I find my rest in you.

Let me flow with the life
that you have given me,
rising and falling,
taking in and letting go,
not clinging to one or the other,
but seeing each as a part of the whole.

Prayers are not only words that are chosen because they seem right or holy sounding. Prayers can also be the feelings we have that embarrass us or seem wrong because they display our weaknesses. They can be feelings of helplessness that desperately whisper, "Help me!" They can be hard anger that asks, "Why did this happen?" They can be loneliness that pleads, "Someone, please love me!" They can be depression when we are empty and must ask, "What is it all about?"

The best prayers are forged in the depths of our being: the prayers we cannot hold back, the ones that spring from the sheer needs of our humanness.

—◅◦▻—

Such prayers are always answered.
Be it here or there,
now or later,
this world or the next.
Such prayers are always answered.

Sooner or later doesn't life call every reflective believer to wrestle with the problem of God and suffering?

RICHARD J. HAUSER
Finding God in Troubled Times

—◄o►—

Why is this happening to me?
Where is God when I cry and pray
and ask for help?
Why does God allow so much suffering?

I don't understand, and I feel angry.
I don't even want to pray anymore.

How can God love me
and still allow me to feel so bad?

Nobody can give me answers;
I have to keep searching for my own.
I hope this isn't all for nothing.

I hope that even my searching is a prayer.

There is no worse suffering than to be a creature. We are like a word which one never finishes pronouncing, eternally suspended and uncertain about its own meaning. A word which does not hear the voice which pronounces it. A word which must be content to let itself be pronounced.

Or else we are like rough-casts that escaped from the hands of our modeler.

We are sick and tired of being hurt, of blows, scrapings, cuttings, remodelings. But when we stop in our furious flight, we find ourselves miserable, terribly insufficient, incapable of expressing ourselves and of finding our bearings, and we cry with anger and indignation against him who is responsible for it.

There is no rest, for a creature, except in the hands of his creator. He alone can complete it, free it from its anxiety and its distress. But the place of its completion is also the place of its pain, the place where God is at work on it.

Louis Evely
Suffering

You have seen many things,
but not observed them;
your ears are open, but you do not hear.

ADAPTED FROM ISAIAH 42:20

—◄o►—

Life does not look the same when we suffer
as it does when we're feeling well.
Feeling well makes us forget who we are,
where we have come from,
and where we are going.

Suffering pushes us to see clearly
and to remember.

Dear God, open my eyes and ears.
Let the lessons of my suffering today
enrich and enliven every aspect
of the journey of my life.

We know that all things work together for good for those who love God.

ROMANS 8:28

—◦—

Too often I see my life as unconnected bits and pieces. Too often I conclude that everything is random. I feel as though you are not thinking of me, ever-present God, not hearing me, but leaving me to chaos and confusion.

At other times I think you are angry with me and that I have lost your care by my sins and neglect. Or I think you are busy with more serious things, oblivious to me and my little life.

Yet all the while you are there, working in my life, weaving it together, interested in my good. Sometimes your grace helps me to see that my luxuries cannot satisfy, that I need to let my poverty make me trust you instead of material things. My health teaches me of your goodness, and my sickness reminds me that I am only here for a while. Your grace opens my eyes to higher goods, and challenges my priorities.

Whatever comes to me, you want to turn to my greater good. Can I believe in a God who is that interested in me, that loving? Dare I?

What if, for just a little while,
I don't fight my sickness
or my discomfort?
What if I just let it be?

What if I don't see it as my enemy,
but recognize it simply
as the way things are for me right now?

What if I reflect on my own integral part
in this universe,
where every person, every tree and plant,
every animal and being is born,
grows and flourishes, diminishes and dies?

If I believe that this universe is created
and sustained by One
who is aware of every sparrow that falls,
who has numbered every hair of our heads,
I might trust such a One,
who holds me always
in great and infinite tenderness.

My child, when you are ill, do not delay,
but pray to [God who] will heal you.

SIRACH 38:9

—◦—

My healing God, I want to be well. I'm so grateful for your gifts of health and wholeness. And I ask you now to bring me back to such a place in my own life. I thank you in advance for hearing my prayer.

Even as I pray, my loving God, I know that you may answer me in ways of which I am not aware. You may heal me in body, or you may choose to extend your healing to places beyond my asking. You know who I am and what I need for my own wholeness. You know the hidden places in me that cry out for your love and attention. I trust that you are already at work in me, bringing healing and blessing in your own ways of wisdom.

The seeds of wisdom, peace, and wholeness are within each of our difficulties.

JACK KORNFIELD
A Path With Heart

—◀◦▶—

O God of wisdom, I never dreamed that illness might offer me such good things. Yet I know you speak through the circumstances of life, and that anywhere you are, there are gifts for me. Help me to cultivate the seeds of these gifts. Create in me the delight and anticipation of one who knows the giver has treasures to offer. What are you offering me, what are your gifts for me in this moment and this illness of my life? Am I willing to do my part, to keep searching for them?

Pain is God's megaphone to rouse a deaf world. Why must it be pain? Why can't He wake us more gently, with violins or laughter? Because the dream from which we must be awakened is the dream that all is well.

Now that is the most dangerous illusion of them all. Self-sufficiency is the enemy of salvation. If you are self-sufficient, you have no need of God. If you have no need of God, you do not seek Him. If you do not seek Him, you will not find Him.

God loves us, so He makes us the gift of suffering. Through suffering, we release our hold on the toys of this world, and know our true good lies in another world.

We're like blocks of stone, out of which the sculptor carves the forms of men. The blows of His chisel, which hurt us so much, are what make us perfect. The suffering in the world is not the failure of God's love for us; it is that love in action.

For believe me, this world that seems to us so substantial is no more than the shadowlands. Real life has not begun yet.

WILLIAM NICHOLSON
Shadowlands

It is Christ Jesus…who indeed intercedes for us. Who will separate us from the love of Christ? Will hardship, or distress, or persecution, or famine, or nakedness, or peril, or sword?

ROMANS 8:34–35

—◄○►—

Wherever we are, God is.

Whatever is going on in our body,
in our mind,
in our spirit,
God is in it with us.

Nothing can separate us from God,
who is closer to us than we are to ourselves.

All-knowing God,
if I am healthy of body,
but sick in my soul,
what does it profit?
If I can see people and nature,
but am blind to their Maker,
what does it profit?
If I can walk or run,
but do not come to you,
what does it profit?
If I recuperate from surgery,
but not from selfishness,
what does it profit?
If I can move with ease,
but am rigid and unloving,
what does it profit?

—◄○►—

All-loving God, heal me in all ways.
Help me be whole physically
and spiritually.
As I ask you to heal my body,
heal also my soul.
For if I am healed only for this world,
what does it profit me?

Illness forces us out of our ruts, trips us up, and challenges us to think about our life. When things are running smoothly, our attention is usually caught by everyday problems and circumstances. Deep thoughts occupy our mind only rarely. We live on "automatic pilot" carried along by others and by all the things we must do.

When sickness brings a threat or an inconvenience, we are thrown off balance. These are the times when we are most likely to come out from behind the mask of our everyday existence. We become ready to open ourselves to the bigger lessons life is offering. Sickness can be a wonderful time to think about ourselves, to reflect on what we are doing and why, to get behind our masks and discover who we are.

—◄o►—

O God who wants to rouse me to a keener awareness of life, wake me up. Let me open up the borders of my everyday sight. Let me look inside as well as outside of myself in expanded ways. Thank you for the ways this illness shakes me up. It pushes me into a clearer awareness of how I limit myself, and of what a great gift life is. Let this new awareness be my avenue to growth in you.

You are standing on holy ground.

EXODUS 3:5

—◄o►—

When I'm sick or suffering from an illness, am up-set, or struggling in my life, I'm always working hard to move away from it, to feel better, or be healed.

Maybe, though, before I move anywhere else, my dear God, I might try to wake up to the impor-tance of where I am. Maybe when I'm sick I am more in touch with what really matters in life. This expe-rience takes me to the heart of why I'm here. This truly is holy ground.

And I see now that every step of my life has been on holy ground. My problem is that when I feel good, I don't even think about the holiness all around and within me.

Dear God, help me to be aware of your pres-ence in this illness. Help me wake up to the holy ground on which I am always standing, no matter what.

Heaven this is not.
Earth it is, the place not yet perfect;
the place of struggling wills,
tainted love,
fragile bodies.
Earth it is, where all is not yet
as we deeply desire;
where we are weak,
when we want to be strong;
lonely, when we yearn to be loved;
sick, when we seek invulnerability
and health.
Earth it is, the road to heaven;
where we become strong by effort
and grace,
where love grows true in time,
where health in soul is more crucial
than perfect bodies.
Earth it is, the promise of heaven;
the hint of what can be,
the slow opening of hearts to others
and God,
the soul becoming whole through
vulnerability.
Heaven, it is not.
But heaven follows.

My brothers and sisters,
whenever you face trials of any kind,
consider it nothing but joy,
because you know that the testing
of your faith produces endurance;
and let endurance have its full effect,
so that you may be mature and complete,
lacking in nothing.

JAMES 1:2–4

◄○►

Dear God,
How hard it is to think of trials and
    difficult times
    as anything to be joyful about.
This is where I have to struggle
    to make my thoughts like yours.
So give me an extra boost in
    my difficulties.
Help me to see the opportunity in each one.

Spirit of health and wholeness,
why do you let me be sick?

† *That you might know my strength,*
and let me make you whole.

But when I am sick,
I do not feel whole and sufficient,
I feel in need.

† *Self-sufficiency is a spiritual sickness*
from which one is often cured during
physical sickness.
You become more whole
by the awareness and acceptance
of your need.

How does seeing my need make me whole?

† *It reveals truth:*
that you are a mortal human, not God,
and that your time here is limited.
It shows how much you need others—
and they need you.
It helps you to see the priorities of life
and encourages you to seek them.
Your need points the way to fulfillment.

Sometimes becoming sick can be a subtle occurrence of our own choosing. When life seems overwhelming, the future unsure, expectations great, and responsibilities too heavy, we seek a temporary escape. It is not that we are pretending to be sick, our "down" attitude can actually affect our immunity, and we become ill, we "catch" something. And illness gives us a legitimate reason to rest, withdraw from others, be left alone, and catch our breath. It serves as an act of survival that we have found effective.

At such times, gracious God, we do not need physical healing as much as inner healing. We seek your grace to deal with life more realistically. We need strength to say no to more requests when we have said yes to enough already. We need your wisdom to be wise enough to balance our time between attending to our own needs and serving the needs of others. We need humility to acknowledge our limitations—that we can do some things, but not all things.

Help us to see that today is enough to handle, without carrying worries for tomorrow. When we can do this, health will dwell both inside and outside ourselves. Grant us this gift, for each of us, for all of us.

O ever-present God,

When my life is fine,
     I forget you.

When sickness comes,
     I entreat you.

When sickness stays,
     I question you.

When death knocks,
     I am angered.

When death is ended,
     I am perfected by you.

May I entrust myself to you
     through all that comes.

I just don't feel good.
I just don't feel good,
and it changes everything.
Usually I can go on doing what
I have to do,
breezing through life feeling comfortable.

But I can't do that now.
I'm so aware that I don't feel good,
and it colors my whole day.
I'm focused on myself
and on my helplessness to change things.
No matter how many pills I take,
or what I do,
I can't change things.

Maybe, God, this is just what I need
once in a while.
Maybe I need something to trip me up
and push me to think,
to broaden and expand my awareness.
Maybe my whole life would "breeze"
by before I realized its passing.
Maybe my whole life would
pass unpondered
unless something interrupted me
and my routine.

A reality break. A wake-up call.
God, let me find you here,
and let me find me here.

Lead, kindly Light,
amid the encircling gloom,
   Lead thou me on.
The night is dark,
and I am far from home,
   Lead thou me on.
Keep thou my feet; I do not ask to see
the distant scene;
one step enough for me.
I was not ever thus, nor prayed that thou
   Shouldst lead me on.
I loved to choose and see my path;
but now
   Lead thou me on.

CARDINAL JOHN HENRY NEWMAN

I have no claim on your healing, creator God. I am a human, and I know we all become ill and suffer at times. Shall I be exempt from my humanness and everyone else bound by it?

Yet, still I pray. I pray because of your goodness, not mine. I believe that you show your power in our weakness, your love in the midst of our needs.

If it be your will, heal me, bolster my faith, and show your power. Make me whole again. And if my physical healing is not your will for me, then show forth your power and love by giving me the strength to accept my condition. Make me accepting and strong in my weakness.

In some ways, dear God,
being sick isn't so bad,
as long as I'm not terribly sick.
Being sick gives me some time off:
time to lie around and take care of myself,
time to read, time to be excused
from some of the tasks and
responsibilities of every day.

Maybe it's bringing a gift for me,
pushing me out of my everyday ruts,
to approach life a little differently.
Perhaps I don't have to wait for sickness
so that I can take time
to love and appreciate and care for myself,
to think different thoughts
and to break out of my usual mind-set,
to stand back and examine
my responsibilities and tasks,
and re-choose what's important.

Along with healing my body, my dear God,
I ask you to give me the Spirit
to grow and to heal in all the dimensions
    of my life.

O God of mystery, I am so influenced by the ways of the world that I want to treat you as we tend to treat one another. As I pray, I feel the desire to barter or make a deal with you. "Cure me and I will pray every morning," I offer. Or, "Make me well and I'll contribute generously to the poor."

O infinite God, do I think you have a price? Do I think I need to convince you to care for me? Perhaps I do not know you, O God of love. I need not buy your love and concern. Like a waterfall, your love falls on me constantly. I need only become aware of it and count on it.

Those who are awake live in a state of constant amazement.

JACK KORNFIELD
Buddha's Little Instruction Book

—◄○►—

Something remarkable has happened
with my illness, my dear God.
Everything about me in this world
has become more beautiful,
more touching!
The sky has never looked so blue.
Even the rain on my window sparkles.
And the dearest of people and creatures
surround me.
Along with my worsening condition
has come
a growing sense of the greatness
of your gifts.
I have been alive in a universe filled
with you,
and my eyes are now beginning to see.
My heart fills up with praise for you,
my God.
"How great thou art!"

If the only prayer you say in your whole life is "thank you," that would suffice.

MEISTER ECKHART

—◄○►—

I must admit, O God, with your grace my illness is teaching me. For even though I still pray to you for the big miracle of my healing, I am already experiencing many little miracles.

My family is closer than ever before; many past hurts with others are mended; genuine concern comes from the unlikeliest of people; and cards and messages convey more love and support than I have ever known.

Within me I find a serenity and trust in you that I never had before. Instead of hurrying, I am able to appreciate even the little things of life, like a solitary bird on the line, rain running down a windowpane, the rustle of wind in the trees. And though I ask for healing, at the same time I feel I must say, "Thanks!"

You are a great and good God. Thank you for all that is good and beautiful, and for your blessings that come with surprise and often in disguise.

The longest journey is the journey inwards.

DAG HAMMARSKJÖLD
Markings

◄○►

Most of the time our energy, thoughts, and efforts are flowing out—out into the events of life, the words of others, the tasks and interests of the world outside us. Sickness blocks some of that flow. It turns our thoughts inward. It raises concerns about our own well-being. It leads us to think self-reflective thoughts, to become more aware that there is an untraveled road winding down, down within us to our very core.

It is the longest journey we will ever make, if we travel this road. And the most important. For on this road, we will discover two magnificent beings: the person we really are, and the God in whose image we are made.

Each morning we are born again.
What we do today is what matters most.

JACK KORNFIELD
Buddha's Little Instruction Book

—◄○►—

Along with many other people in this world
    whom I don't even know,
I'm living this day with the experience
    of illness.
Though it may not be what I would choose,
    it's what has chosen me.
I'm sharing in the suffering of this world.

How can I take what I was "born with"
    this day
    and find fullness of life?
How can I find wholeness in sickness?
How can I join my own discomfort
    and distress
    with that of all others suffering
    throughout the world?
How can I walk together with them
    toward healing?

My God, may my new birth today, and my experience of this day with all that it holds, join me with all other sufferers, and bring us all closer to our wholeness in you.

31

God said, "Do not fear, greatly beloved, you are safe. Be strong and courageous!"

DANIEL 10:19

—◄○►—

Faithful God, soon I will have an operation. I pray that you guide the hands and minds of the doctors and nurses. Help them to bring your healing to me. I am very aware of how much I must trust them and leave myself in their skillful hands.

Yet you are more real than they. You have more interest in me than they ever can. As they gather around my body and reach out to help me, may I also feel your presence and the touch of your peace. As I entrust myself to them, I entrust myself even more to you.

The God of love says:

† *My people, there are not two,*
but three answers to prayer:
Yes! No! and Wait!

Yes! At times you are so attuned to my will, that what
you ask of me is exactly what I want for you. Some-
times I give without your asking. At other times, ask-
ing increases your openness and the recognition of our
relationship. It helps you to realize that you are my
creature and I am your Lord.

No! Though you see something as being for your good
and happiness, I may see that it is not so. My provi-
dence may see it as a peril, a danger to your life with
me. I cannot say yes when my love says no.

Wait! Time is a great teacher. Time is needed for
growth and to reach wholeness. "Wait until you grow
up," you say to your children. I say the same to mine.
The frustration of not being immediately gratified, of
asking, waiting, and still hoping often leads to much
wisdom.

God, you search me and know me.
You know if I am standing or sitting.
You perceive my thoughts from far away.
Whether I walk or lie down,
    you are watching;
you are familiar with all my ways.

· · · · · · ·

You know me through and through
from having watched my bones take shape
when I was being formed in secret,
woven together in the womb.
You have seen my every action;
all were recorded in your book.

PSALM 139:1–3, 15–16
Psalms Anew

So God, you know exactly
    what is happening within me.
You know it better than I do,
    better than my doctor does.
I am not alone in my pain, in my worry,
    in any of my distress.
When I feel sad about my situation,
when I worry about what I have to face,
when I feel weak and without energy,
when I can't think straight,
you are here with me.
You created me
    and walk every step of my life with me.
I know you will be with me
    faithfully to the end.

I will lead the blind
    by a road they do not know,
by paths they have not known
    I will guide them.
I will turn the darkness before them
       into light,
    the rough places into level ground.
These are the things I will do,
    and I will not forsake them.

Isaiah 42:16

We are so blind to the ways of God. We expect God's ways to be like our ways, God's route to be the path we would choose. We tend to have only today's comfort in mind. God is mindful of eternal joy. We curse the crookedness and darkness of ambiguity in our life. We do not know how it leads into the brilliant purpose of divine light. While often objecting, we are led by the grace of God along the way of true growth and sincere holiness. Thanks be to you, faithful and guiding God.

Are not two sparrows sold for a penny? Yet not one of them will fall to the ground apart from [God]. And even the hairs of your head are all counted. So do not be afraid; you are of more value than many sparrows.

MATTHEW 10:29–31

—◄o►—

What is a bird worth, my God? Not much in our markets, where life is cheap. But with you, all you have made is of worth.

What am I worth to you, my God? The living and dying of Jesus proves I am priceless to you.

You love me more than I love myself, and you constantly watch over every aspect of my life. You are fully aware of my illness.

As I struggle with it, help me trust in your provident care.

When you finally awake, you don't try to make good things happen; they just happen. You understand suddenly that everything that happens to you is good.

ANTHONY DE MELLO
Awareness

━◦━

How hard it is to think of illness as good, when our usual way of looking at things sees it as bad, as undesirable, as worthy of avoidance. How can we come to think anything good about illness? Perhaps we need to examine our ideas of *good*. Do they come from our world's idea of good, or from the life, death, and resurrection of Jesus? The reality of illness may be one of the important areas in which our way of thinking and believing is challenged, up to the moment when we are able to see God working in everything, and thus can call illness truly good.

O God, you are total goodness and exist in every circumstance. Help me find you everywhere. Help me find you in places I never would have thought to look for you. Show me your presence in my suffering and my difficult times. Let these times, as miserable as they are, be the place where I find you, cling to you, and come to new life in you.

I am not greater than you, my God. If I do not like to see those I love suffer, shall I believe you do?

If I can understand the tears and apprehension of children sitting in the dentist's chair or being immunized by a doctor, and know the future good that comes from those unpleasant moments, can I not believe you see a future good for me out of this time of my suffering and tears?

If I can watch students and athletes struggle in hard times, knowing the struggle is indispensable for their growth and success, do I not suspect you see in my struggles with illness an even greater promise of growth and success?

I am not greater than you, my God. Yet from my limited understanding and compassion for those in my world, help me glimpse a hint of your understanding and compassion, which are infinite, mysterious, and more universal than I can fathom. Then let me trust your wisdom and compassion more than my own.

A powerful wind came, but God did not come with it. After the wind came an earthquake, but God was not in the earthquake either. Then fire came, but God was not in the fire.

Finally, when the fire left, God's voice came in the silence.

ADAPTED FROM KINGS 19:11–13

Gracious God, most of the time my life is filled with wind, earthquakes, and fire. There is much action, chattering, wall-to-wall words, radio and television, family problems, and occasional crises. I work too much, hurry too often, worry exceedingly. It is no wonder I miss your voice and think of you as far away and uninvolved in my life.

But now I am sick. My illness causes me to focus more on myself and on you. It muffles the noise of the world. My illness leads me into a silence where you speak. Before I fall asleep, or after I awake in the quiet of the night, silence accompanies me. When I am alone in the car or on a walk, silence accompanies me. Help me not to run from it, for you have much to tell me with your certain, calm voice.

Maybe one of the things my illness will teach me is the value of silence. I understand now why a very old man once said, "All my teachers are dead now, except silence."

Be still and know that I am God." Many are not sure of God because they are never quiet. From time to time, they should ask for a hush to life to lose the voices of the world. The voice of God is heard only in quiet.

FULTON J. SHEEN
Simple Truths

You might try, just as an experiment, to hold yourself in awareness and acceptance for a time…as a mother would hold a hurt or frightened child, with a completely available and unconditional love.

JON KABAT-ZINN
Wherever You Go, There You Are

—◄○►—

Sometimes when we're sick, we add to our problem by being harsh with ourselves, by blaming ourselves for our condition or being angry that we've become so weak or helpless. Such criticism and punishment do not help.

Instead of being critical, take a few moments to be gentle and loving. Imagine holding your own ailing self, with all your pain and fear, in a deep caring and attention. Extend to yourself compassion and blessing, as you enter into God's deep and personal love for you.

> Can a woman forget her nursing child,
>> or show no compassion for the child
>> of her womb?
> Even these may forget,
>> yet I will not forget you.
> See, I have inscribed you on the palms
>> of my hands.

ISAIAH 49:15–16

Finding [God] in the constant personal awareness of the world he has created around us and within us is the…secret liturgy of the universe [that] unites us to the source of all being with every breath we take and every word we utter in our daily surrender to life.

ANTHONY DE MELLO
as quoted in Carlos G. Valles, Mastering Sadhana

◄o►

Sometimes we struggle and battle with life. We want no part of what's going on and thus work with all our might to change things. Illness often presents us with such a struggle.

Sometimes we come to know our struggle is fruitless. Our illness is serving a purpose. It may be providing us with the means to take us on the next step of our journey, our transformation into the next stage of life.

Surrender to life may mean surrender to death. Or it may mean surrender to the next stage of this life, with all that it holds.

Whatever happens, when we surrender to awareness of God's presence in all that is going on around us and in us, we are united with the source of all being.

Sickness may be the solemn occasion of God's intervention in a person's life.

PAUL TORNIER

—◄○►—

Seek not outside yourself,
    for the ceasing of your suffering
    comes from within,
    even while you hold back, defend,
    stand still, and hide.

God has great things in mind for you.
You have given your Creator smaller things,
    self-saving things.
The pressure from God's life
    pushing forward while you hold back
    causes your present inner turmoil
    and pain.
Know now: collaboration will bring
    fulfillment and peace.
Your story, though, is everyone's story.

God urges us to grow.
    We strain to stay secure.
God calls us into the unknown.
    We procrastinate going.
God made our souls expandable.
    We feel we will break.
God says, "Now!"
    We say, "Wait!"

The God we think of as silent
    is always speaking and urging.
The Spirit is teaching
    where true happiness lies.
If we are to reach it, find it, feel it,
    we need to go through the pain
    to come out on the other side,
    into the free, fresh air of Christ's peace.
This takes time, listening,
    and much understanding—
    sometimes more than we want
    to give ourselves.
So we settle for the pain.

I am angry at you, God! I lived a good life and followed your law. Yet you have permitted my sickness and suffering.

✝ *Were you faithful and moral only to buy a comfortable life for yourself? Or did you choose the good because you loved me and believed it was right?*

I even feel that you have not listened to my prayers. Instead, you remain silent and leave me to my misery and pain. I have prayed for so long and nothing has improved. Why do you not hear me and answer me?

✝ *I respond to you even though I seem silent. I always act based on your greater good. I remain committed to a deep love for you, even when you do not see it.*

How does love permit suffering?

✝ *Do parents reject a vaccination because their child will cry? Do teachers give the answers to save students the struggle of finding them? Should children be kept from leaving home because of the pain of separation?*

God of mercy, as you teach me, help me to trust you, to wait for you, to believe in you while you are guiding me.

My body is so tired, my God. It's wearing out. It has served me well, carrying me through this world with great care and service. And now I know that my bones and muscle and all my substance are weakened by the inevitable passage of time.

I thank you for my body, for all that it has done for me in this world. I thank you for all the blessings that have come to me through my senses and physical awareness, for the many things I've seen, touched, and known.

I thank you for the strength I've had, for the ability to work and move and do many of the things I've wanted and chosen to do. I thank you too for play and pleasure, for the enjoyment of so many of your tangible gifts.

I thank you for my ability to think, to reason, to appreciate, to be aware. When my time has come, my loving God, receive me and help me to release my body with gratitude and love. Thank you, God, for my body, wonderfully made and gratefully lived in.

If you can be still and suffer awhile, you shall without a doubt see the help of God come in your need.

THOMAS À KEMPIS
Imitation of Christ

—◄○►—

God of healing, God of hope, God of love, heal me as you will and give me hope. You meet me in all my weaknesses and broken places. Those are the spots where I am most vulnerable, least able to defend or protect myself. Yet that's where you find entry. Help me to know your wholeness and power and love there. Let me realize that you are there waiting for me. May my helplessness challenge me to find strength and healing in you.

That evening, at sundown, they brought to him all who were sick or possessed with demons. And the whole city was gathered around the door.

MARK 1:32–33

—◦—

We humans divide ourselves into the healthy and the sick. But the truth is, saving God, we are all in need of your healing. The whole town—the whole world—needs to stand at your door and ask to be cured. We too often fail to recognize our illness.

We readily diagnose cancer, heart disease, and emphysema; less easily do we become aware of our greed, envy, or pride. We recognize the presence of arthritis, alcoholism, or diabetes, yet we don't recognize the demons of busyness, materialism, or hate that we permit to possess us.

Before I reach the sundown of my life, help me see myself honestly. As I now pray and ask you to cure my body, I ask just as earnestly that you cure my soul. May your grace make me the whole, holy person you call me to be. Then with a clean heart I can ask you to cure my body and make me sound, through and through.

I have loved you with an everlasting love.

JEREMIAH 31:3

—◀o▶—

Note the word *everlasting*.
For God, it has no qualifiers.
That means God says to us:

✝ *I have loved you when you behaved kindly*
and were very loving.
I have loved you when you behaved terribly.
I have loved you when you were well
and beautiful.
I have loved you when you were sick
and looked awful.
I have loved you when you were very,
very good.
I have loved you when you were horrid.

God says,

✝ *Not "because" of anything do I love you. My love*
creates your very being.

Whether I am well or sick,
may I rest in the assurance
of your love, my God.

Thou Christ of God,
   who brought
   dead Lazarus
   from the tomb,
Stand also
   before these living graves
   and command us,
   by thy power,
   to
   come forth!

WILLIAM T. JOYNER
Wheels in the Air

Living God,
May I live my life until it's very end.
May I never be caught in tombs
   of my own making.
May I always be willing to be called forth.

I look at others,
    at the health and strength
    of their bodies.
I hear their laughter,
    their plans for tomorrow.
Then I look at myself,
    my sickness and misery,
    my uncertain future
    and I wonder, my God,
    "Why me?"

Then, my God, you respond
    to my wondering,
    and you ask me:

✝ *Why not?*
Why are others to be touched
    by the infirmities of life,
    and not you?
Why should you avoid suffering
    and the struggle
    of making sense of it all?
Why shouldn't you be as human as they?

And I cannot answer. I have no special right to exemption, no claim to a life free from sorrow or misfortune. Forgive me my naiveté and my pride. With a humility born of this truth, I can only ask of you, if it be your will, heal me. If it is time for me to learn and grow, help me with your strength.

For my thoughts are not your thoughts,
nor are your ways my ways.

ISAIAH 55:8

—◄o►—

My God, I'm just realizing that I don't know you! My image of you is coming apart as I struggle with my sickness. I thought that if I believed and trusted you, you would save me from suffering. I thought that if I prayed and lived a good life, I would be special to you, and your love would protect me. And now I'm suffering, scared, and I don't know where you are!

† *My precious one, I'm closer to you than you are to yourself. You try to capture me in your own ways, but your image of me is far too small and limiting.*

I know your belief and trust in me, and I forget none of your struggles and efforts. This illness invites you to grow and to expand your image and awareness of me.

I want you to begin to experience me in places you've never seen me before, because I'm there!

I want you to find me in the darkness as well as in the light, because I'm there! I want you to seek me in your illness, in your pain, and in your failing body, because I'm there!

I want you to sense my presence when you feel most alone, because I'm there! Stretch and expand, my beloved, I'm asking you to grow.

Can a woman forget her nursing child,
or show no compassion for the child
of her womb?
Even these may forget,
yet I will not forget you.

ISAIAH 49:15

—◄○►—

O God, for too long I have thought of you only as a distant and severe being. How comforting it is to hear your warm words to me through the prophet Isaiah. How consoling to know that you are more concerned for me than the most loving mother.

Take me in your arms as I struggle with my illness. Hold me close to you so that I may sense your presence. Support me by the realization that I am at this moment in your mind. You attend to me constantly. You tell me that you notice every tear of mine and every fear. No struggle is insignificant.

When I feel alone, remind me of my importance to you. When I am worried, help me hear the heartbeat of your love for me. When I feel fragile or hopeless, remind me that I am your offspring and that the children of God will one day be strong and glorious, and will live forever with you.

Despair is the twin of pessimism.
It says that today is bad,
    tomorrow will be worse.
It survives on cynicism,
    and snickers at words
    of encouragement.
Despair is a thief
    who steals away our hope.

Hope is the twin of optimism.
It says that sickness, suffering, and death
    will never win out.
It trusts in One who loves,
    and believes God's promises
    of better tomorrows.
Hope is a prophet who says
    that all that we really long for
    will come true.

Despair and hope compete for our mind.
Our thoughts tell us which one is winning.

Listen to me…you whom I have
brought to birth,
and carried since the time you were born.
When your hair is gray,
I shall still support you.
As I have already done for you,
so will I do.
I have carried you,
I have taught you to walk.
In your old age,
I shall still support and deliver you.
I will be your God.

ADAPTED FROM ISAIAH 46:3–4, 15

◀◦▶

Let these words of God, spoken to you, lead you into
a quiet reverie. Allow yourself to relax. Close your
eyes and breathe deeply.

When you are ready, bring to mind an image of
yourself as a newborn baby. Imagine yourself rest-
ing in the arms of your strong and loving God, who
is looking on you with great warmth and delight.
God is holding you close and smiling at you! Stay
with that image of yourself in God's arms.

Gradually allow other pictures of your life to
come into your mind—times of childhood, events
of your youth. See yourself walking to school, play-
ing with your friends, at home with your family. As
you see yourself, imagine your God of love and care

being close beside you, watching over you every step of your journey, enjoying time with you.

Move through images of your growing up, as you made your way into and through the world. Recall times of work and times of delight. See yourself as you made friends and connected with people who became significant in your adult life. Again, imagine God who loves you standing close by in all of these times, loving and supporting you.

Finally, move together with this God into your present situation. With your eyes still closed, imagine your God sitting at your bedside. Or imagine God supporting you as you walk. See yourself leaning on God, who bears you up and gives you strength.

Hold this image in your mind. Know that the God who brought you to birth and continues to love you is still with you. That God has walked every step of your life with you and delights in you. Your God knows your present pain and worry and distress, and yet, even today says to you,

† *I shall still support and deliver you.*

For God's foolishness is wiser than human wisdom, and God's weakness is stronger than human strength.

1 CORINTHIANS 1:25

━◄○►━

How can you be so foolish, almighty God, to create us as strong and healthy beings and then permit us to become sick and weak? Why do you make us so marvelous, with quick and clever minds, and then over time let us become slow and forgetful? Is that not foolish? Or is there some great wisdom to the foolishness that we think we see in you? Is there an exquisite plan you ask us to trust?

How can you be so weak, almighty God? Why do you let disease have its way with us? When you do not cure the people you have made, is that not a sign of your weakness, a powerlessness, and a yielding to illness? Or is there a strength that you will show when you free us from all illness and death? Is there a brilliant glory still to come?

Help us, O God, to trust in your foolishness and rely on your weakness.

When I am feeling depressed,
it can be from three possible sources.
It is possible that certain chemicals
in my body are in disarray.
A physician for my body can help me.

Or it could be that I am depressed
because the feelings of my heart
are sore and confused
by the experiences of my life.
A psychologist can help me understand
and accept my feelings.

Or it could be that
I feel sadness in my soul
because I have not chosen well or lived well.
God, the physician of my soul, can help me
with forgiveness, peace, and love,
and a chance to start over anew.

Help me, my God,
to find the way to life again.

We might…discover that depression has its own angel, a guiding spirit whose job it is to carry the soul away to its remote places where it finds unique insight and enjoys a special vision.

THOMAS MOORE
Care of the Soul

◄○►

It's hard to think that anything good can come from depression, my dear God. It feels like such a dark place of aloneness, with no way out. But perhaps special treasures are hidden in the darkest places, waiting for those who begin the journey and enter the darkness. Let me find the gifts hidden for me there. Give me the "special vision" to see you in these places where I least expected to find you.

Faith is the bird
    that sings to the dawn
    while it is still dark.
Because I believe in you, my God,
I will keep singing
    in the darkness of my life.

Though I cannot see it now,
    I believe the dawn will come;
though I cannot find
    the right melody of joy,
I will sing a song of my trust in you.

And when I finally see the soft glow
    of a new day coming,
I will know all the more
    that you are the God
    who always keeps promises.

Darkness seems to be everywhere, my God, inside of me and all around. Help me to know that you are the God of darkness as well as of light. Even though I may not feel your presence, I trust that you are near. Sit with me in this darkness. Help me to find you here. Help me to find all the gifts that are hidden here for me.

Just when the caterpillar
    thought the world was over,
    it became a butterfly.
For me, too, Lord,
    it is not easy to tell the difference
    between moments of dying
    and moments of new birth.
Help me to trust in you
    and your plans for me.
You are always working in my life
    accomplishing great things
    in mysterious ways.
You encourage me
    as you say to me in Scripture:
✝ *"See, I am doing something new!"*
    Now it springs forth,
    Do you not perceive it?

Demon Suffering, why do you afflict the world so? More than any other demon, you lead us to question the existence of God. You whisper to us, "If God really existed and was loving and good, God wouldn't let you suffer so. God is imaginary, only a wish. There is only you and this world."

Demon Suffering, your logic is persuasive, your reasoning clever. I am often tempted to believe you, yet something within me intervenes. I cannot see my God, but I sense God's presence. I cannot fathom God's reasons, but I believe and I trust. Though I am confused by your existence, O Suffering, I suspect that even in you I can find my mysterious and provident God.

Demon Suffering, you may deride me for being gullible, you may laugh at me for my faith, as some laugh at love. But faith and love are larger than reason, greater than logic. Because of them, I know even you, O Suffering, will lose your power to harm or destroy me. For when I believe in God's engendering love for me, you are the one who is conquered, O Demon Suffering. After the sufferings of this life, God's glory will shine forth in me.

In the Hebrew Scriptures, God tells Moses how to call down a blessing. Among these instructions are the words:

"May God's face be uncovered to you."

ADAPTED FROM NUMBERS 6:25

◄○►

In our sicknesses, when we feel a great need for God's help and blessing, when we feel God is absent, or when we have trouble finding where God is, we might use such a prayer for ourselves. God said that when such words are used, "I will bless them" (Numbers 6:27).

When I feel all alone and cannot find you,
O God, uncover your face to me.

When my body is failing,
    and I'm growing weak and helpless,
O God, uncover your face to me.

When I find myself in darkness
    and don't know how
    to make my way out,
O God, uncover your face to me.

When I just need to know you are here,
O God, uncover your face to me
    and bless me.

I look healthy to others, but I am sick, Lord. I have the illness of depression. I feel empty and alone, and I just don't care. I don't care about my work or the things that other people enjoy. I feel life is passing me by while I sit outside it. I seem to be separated from life and from others by an impenetrable glass wall. I can look through and see warmth, enthusiasm, and sociability on the other side. On my side there is only numbness, dryness, and loneliness. I even feel you, O God, are on the other side of the wall. Help me! Please!

—◄○►—

† *Walls can be removed, doors can be built, openings are eventually found, medical and spiritual attention is nearby. There is no thing or mood in this world that is permanent, only me, your God. I did not make you to be imprisoned in the numbness of depression. I am working all the while to lead you to fullness and life. Sometimes your path will lead you through dark or empty valleys. In those times, do your part, then watch for me, wait for me, listen, and you will hear me speak. I will lead you out. Follow me. I will lead you into the bright joy of life.*

Learn to let go. That is the key to happiness.

JACK KORNFIELD
Buddha's Little Instruction Book

—◄○►—

Dear God, I do so well at connecting and holding on. So many precious gifts are part of my life, and I'm so grateful. I love them all: the people who are so dear, my home, my work, all the things I love to do, my treasures, my health, and my life. How hard it is when the time comes to let go of any of them! And yet I know that nothing in this world stays forever.

Teach me to let go, to hold what I love with open hands. When the time comes for me to release any of your gifts—my health, my positions in life, anything dear—hold me close as I give them back to you with love and gratitude. Be with me then in the grief and sadness that are so much a part of my letting go.

Who are you, God?
Who are you, who lets us suffer so?
Who are you, who bids us to pray,
     then seems so silent?
Who are you
     who allows the path to be so
     uncertain?

✝ *Who are you,*
who knows not your creaturehood?
Who are you,
who will not look beyond suffering?
Who are you,
who will not enter into silence and hear me?
Who are you,
so afraid of the path unless you clear it?

Who are you?
You are the one I love and made.
You are the one I am leading home.
You are the one who will someday
know me well and be glad!

Happy experiences make life delightful; painful experiences lead to growth. This does not mean that we are to seek suffering and provoke pain.…But it does mean that we must use suffering when it comes for this noble purpose. Don't let the chance pass. Never say, "When this suffering passes, I'll be happy again." No. If you are not happy with things as they are with you now, you'll never be.

ANTHONY DE MELLO
quoted by Carlos G. Valles in Mastering Sadhana

—◦—

My God, I don't understand why it has to be so painful to grow. I want to grow and become all that you created me to be, but don't like or want the pain and suffering. When they come I always feel like I must have done something wrong to bring them on. They feel like punishment.

Help me to change my way of thinking. Let me recognize that my path is like that of all creation: that everything alive comes to birth, grows, eventually weakens, and dies. Help me to see that you are there through all. Help me with the pain.

My mind fails me, living God. The names I can't recall, the word that won't come to mind, the event of yesterday that has vanished without a clue: these things trouble and embarrass me. They trouble and embarrass me a lot. I feel like I'm losing my very self. I feel like I am losing my dignity. I find that I want to hide all these losses, all these moments, from those around me. I even want to hide them from myself.

This is such a difficult part of human aging to accept. Please give me the humility and courage I need to accept them. Help me to realize my value does not come from the quickness of my mind, the recall of my memory, the strength of my body, or the features of my face.

My value comes from my person, the person you have made. I am created in your image and loved by you. As my vigor of mind and body subsides, help me become even more aware of myself as this wonderful person you have created—and for whose heart you long.

Gracious God, the body you gave me is wearing out. My illness is not a passing disease. My illness is my humanness. I would like so much to be divine, to be invulnerable, forever strong and healthy, with no limited time in which to live. Isn't this the desire we expressed in Eden?

But I am not a god. You are God, and I am your creature. You have made me a most noble creature in all the universe, a mixture of earth and heaven, dust and breath of God. There comes a time when each dimension returns to its origin, dust to dust, breath to God. May I accept this process not as an annihilation, but as a fulfillment, a coming home.

Though my body weakens, may I respect and accept it, for it is marvelously made by you. And I will endure forever. May I appreciate myself, the distinct person and image of you that I am. May my humanness help me to grow more compassionate to myself and others. Help me to become more wise with an otherworldly wisdom, and to be a believer in the new life to come.

Likewise the Spirit helps us in our weakness; for we do not know how to pray as we ought, but that very Spirit intercedes with sighs too deep for words. And God, who searches the heart, knows what is the mind of the Spirit, because the Spirit intercedes for the saints according to the will of God.

ROMANS 8:26–27

At this very moment,
even when I'm not aware,
the Spirit is within me,
praying for what I need,
and is being heard by God.

At this very moment,
even when I don't know what I need,
what to pray for,
the Spirit does know,
and is asking from the depths of my being,
and God is listening.

At this very moment,
all I need to do is say yes.

Angel of God, my guardian dear,
to whom God's love entrusts me here,
throughout this day be at my side,
to light my way and be my guide.
Amen.

TRADITIONAL

Here dies another day
during which I have had eyes, ears, hands
and the great world around me;
and with tomorrow begins another.
Why am I allowed two?

G. K. CHESTERTON

Even having one day of life is a miraculous gift, O God. Yet, you have already given me more days than I can number. I must admit I have not appreciated their beauty or preciousness. Now I am ill. I long for healthy days again. I pray that you give me many more days and years here in your beautiful world with the people I love. And as the days go by, prepare me as well for the greatest gift to come—the eternal day of heaven that will thrill me forever.

One day, when time is coming to an end, I will look back over my life and all that made it up. I hope that I will see then with a clarity and purpose never before experienced.

With surprise I may see that during my happiest times, though deeply enjoyable, I grew least of all. Good times balanced my life and gave me a zest and vitality, but times of problems, illness, and suffering challenged me, stretched me, and enlarged my soul. The obstacles to a life of ease were catalysts that moved me forward toward more than I could be. As I look back over my life, I may see that without the hard times I would never have become courageous, believing, loving, trusting.

So even though I now ask that you cure me, O ever-present God, I keep this strange paradox of true life in my mind—that the narrow and hard ways lead to life, too. I know that one day I may thank you for this time from which I now seek release. That is why today I place myself in your hands. I say, "If it is your will, heal me; if it is not your will, grant me courage to go forward."

Then Jesus told them a parable about their need to pray always and not to lose heart.

LUKE 18:1

—◄○►—

O God of my life, I need you to teach me how to never lose heart. I pray. I have prayed all my life, and I have always believed in praying. But now that I am so sick, I am beginning to feel like it's all useless.

I ask for healing. Sometimes I just ask to feel better, but nothing happens. I begin to wonder why I even pray. I lose heart.

Maybe something else is happening. Perhaps you hear me and answer me, but the answer is not the one I was expecting or wanting. Will I pray only when I get what I want? How do I know what's in my own best interest? Down deep, I trust you whose wisdom is so far beyond mine, whose love for me knows no bounds. Is this my answer?

In my sickness, gentle God,
    help me remember
    all the good you have given me.
You have created me out of nothingness
    and brought me to life.
You have given me people
    who care for and support me,
    and friends who have chosen me
        out of all the others.
You have given me
    talents of mind and body,
    and a vitality and productiveness
        all my own.
You have led me into loving relationships,
    given me a belief in you,
    and blessed my life
        with frequent happiness.

Because of my illness, shall I now question
    your kindness to me?
Shall I think you have forgotten me?
Shall I think of you as a changeable God
    who has ceased to love me?
No, I cannot.
As I ask that you heal me of my illness,
    gentle God,
I also ask that I never doubt
    your care for me.

Though much is taken, much abides;
and though
We are not now that strength which
in old days
Moved earth and heaven; that
which we are,
we are—
One equal temper of heroic hearts,
Made weak by time and fate,
but strong in will
To strive, to seek, to find, and not to yield.

ALFRED LORD TENNYSON
"Ulysses"

Dear God, remind me of what still abides in me. I've become so aware of how I seem to be failing, that I lose track of what gifts I still have. Help me to be grateful for my strengths, my abilities, all that I've learned in my life, and how I've grown through the years. Sometimes it's good for me to remember and be grateful.

When you see God dancing in everything, then the things you thought were evil or bad no longer seem evil or bad, because God is dancing even in them.

ANDREW HARVEY
The Way of Passion

—◄o►—

God, give me eyes
to see you dancing everywhere,
in all the people and things
I dearly love and enjoy,
as well as in places
I never dreamed you could be.
If I can find you there,
I know I can never be separated from you.
You and I are whirling together,
in sickness and in health,
in the dance of life.

Very truly, I tell you, when you were younger, you used to fasten your own belt and to go wherever you wished. But when you grow old, you will stretch out your hands, and someone else will fasten a belt around you and take you where you do not wish to go."

JOHN 21:18

—◄○►—

Merciful God, I now live the unpleasant aspects of being ill. Besides the sufferings, there are also the limitations, the inability to move about, the inner submission to other people—nurses, doctors, relatives, and caretakers. I cannot drive my car, I must be assisted to walk, I need help to dress and wash. I am taken to unpleasant places for scans, tests, and the scrutiny of my body inside and out. I almost feel like an object or a child again. Help me keep my dignity and a sense of my value as a person.

In my condition I think of you, Christ Jesus, as you were led to your death by others. You kept your dignity and saw some grander picture. You humbly accepted your human limitations and, by your humility, were expanded rather than diminished. Help me to be like you. Help me to submit my will to the harsh demands of life, and be expanded as a person.

Then one day, free of my limitations, bring me to your embrace, where I will receive again strength and joy a thousandfold.

I, your God, offer you the choice of life or death. Choose life."

ADAPTED FROM DEUTERONOMY 30:19

—◄o►—

Life is full of experiences of loss and struggle, and even death. We can't live long before we meet difficulties and losses of many kinds. While often we can't change the experience, we come to see that we do have a choice in how we cope with it. That choice is between finding the life yet to be lived, or settling into bitterness and negativity.

When we're sick, or suffering in some way, or even coming to the end of our lives, the choice is right before us. Do I try to find the life and growth being offered to me in my distress, or do I refuse to make any effort to cope in a healthy way? It's always my choice.

Loving God, who is with us in every part of our lives, help me to choose life whenever I come up against loss, sickness, or even death. I realize that choosing life can be painful and difficult. Yet I know your strength is always here for me. Show me the ways I can healthily choose life, no matter what my circumstances might be.

God, you are my shepherd;
I shall not want.
In verdant pastures you give me repose.
Beside restful waters you lead me;
you refresh my soul.

PSALM 23:1–3
Psalms Anew

—◄o►—

Let the words of this psalm lead you into a peaceful sense of the presence of God, who is with you at this very moment of your illness.

Find, as well as you can, a comfortable position and close your eyes. Take several deep breaths, relaxing more deeply each time you exhale. Ask God to lead you, and in your mind see yourself coming into a beautiful, open field of soft grasses and wildflowers, blue sky, and a sparkling stream. Notice all the things you see and sense around you: trees, a gentle breeze, the warmth of the sun, any animal that may appear.

Be aware that God is with you as you settle down in this lovely setting. Rest quietly in this place for as long as you wish, sensing the near and loving presence of God. Words are not necessary. Just stay in the presence of the One who loves you. If you wish, speak gently of your concerns to the One who is listening.

When you feel your time in such communion is over, slowly and peacefully breathe deeply and open your eyes. Remain in the presence of God. When times become particularly painful or difficult, return to this place of awareness and rest in God's presence.

From meaninglessness in suffering,
    deliver me, O God.
From despair and surrendering of hope,
    deliver me, O God.
From thinking that you are far away,
    deliver me, O God.
From listening too much to my fears,
    deliver me, O God.
From being more anxious about my body
      than my soul,
    deliver me, O God.
From being angry at my weakness,
    deliver me, O God.
From using my illness to manipulate others,
    deliver me, O God.
From denying that a cross can lead to a crown,
    deliver me, O God.
From failing to believe in future glory,
    deliver me, O God.
From a small faith that will not trust,
    deliver me, O God.
From thinking only of myself
      and not of others,
    deliver me, O God.
From taking the kindness of others
      for granted,
    deliver me, O God.
Deliver me, my God, from all the ways
      I can work against myself.
Help me believe in your grace working
      for my good. Amen.

Allow the Lord, by his love and grace, to let you live in this moment. Right now. This moment is as perfect…as it can be.…Just respond to the need that presents itself right in front of you.

RICHARD ROHR
Radical Grace

—◄○►—

When this moment is filled with suffering, pain, worry, and distress, it's difficult to want to be here. We plunge into distractions, or retreat to warm memories of the past.

Yet these are the moments when we tend to be the most vulnerable, the most aware of our need for God. And that very vulnerability and need is a powerful drawing force for the God who waits to be drawn. For this moment is the only place we can find God.

The challenge for us when we're ill is to stay with the sickness, to look for God hidden there. Only then can we begin to open ourselves to that healing power, that life that permeates even our broken times. Perhaps our very need—our sickness—is the magnet that draws God and us together.

O God who waits for me here and now, help me not to flee from you. Let us be in this moment together.

I used to think I knew how to pray,
   my God.
I could say all the right words.
I could praise you.
I thought I knew what to ask for
   and how to ask.
Not that I always got what I wanted.
But at least I thought I knew how to pray.

Things have changed now with my illness.
I've changed.
Sometimes I don't know the words to say,
   though my being wants to say
   something.
Sometimes there simply are no words.
I'm just here.
At other times the words come pouring out,
   and I'm not sure where they come from.
Now I have no idea how to pray.

Maybe what I need to know is that
   there is no set or special way to pray.
Maybe, if I want it to be,
   everything in my life now is a prayer.
Maybe that's what you've wanted from me
   all along.

He was a feisty old man, friendly but feisty. I knew him for about twenty years. He was used to having his own way—aren't we all? One day he came with the bad news that he had prostate cancer. He was determined to beat it, and with expert medical help, he did for several years. But then the cancer returned. Several weeks before he died, he came to see me again. What a changed attitude he had. He said, "I used to always pray that God would cure me; now when I pray I just say, 'Whatever you want.'"

All-good God, how many times have I prayed, "Thy will be done on earth as it is in heaven"? You are always open to my prayers, to the expressions of my will, my wishes, and my wants. Yet even though I ask many things of you, help me be accepting enough of your will that I can silently say with every prayer of mine, "Whatever you want."

I am jittery today, my God of peace.
Help me to settle down.
I get so tired of being sick, of being quiet,
of lying around,
yet I have no ability to do anything else.

Take this unused energy
and convert it into prayer.
These cries of mine
that are pushing their way out,
let them make such a sound all around you
that you will turn to me
in stillness and peace.
Take my jitters, dear God;
give me your quiet and rest.

Has God ever suffered? Does God know anything about pain? Does God know what I suffer? Did God ever have a migraine headache, as if his head was crowned with thorns? Does God know anything about the wounded hands and feet that are brought in to the accident wards of hospitals? Does God know anything about the starvation in India and Africa? Did he ever go without food for two days? or three? or five? Does he know anything about thirst? Does God know anything about homelessness? Was he ever without a home? Does he know what it is to be a refugee? To flee from one country to another? Does he know what it is to be in jail? to be the victim of scourging? Does God know any of these things? Yes. God is in Christ reconciling the world to himself.

FULTON J. SHEEN

I really don't feel like praying to you, God. Because of my illness I am depressed. Then why do I even try to pray? I have heard that you love me; do you love me?

✝ *Yes, I do, more than you know.*

Then why do you let me feel so much sadness?

✝ *At some time or other, all lives are sad and heavy. At other times, they are bright and full of meaning. Life in this world is a mixture of night and day.*

But my life has been dark for so long, and I feel it will never be bright again. Will it?

✝ *I did not make you for sadness, but for joy. I am always leading you there, even through the darkness.*

Give me some sign that you are near, that you love me and are leading me toward the light.

✝ *When you did not feel like praying, I moved you to try to pray, to talk to me anyway. I am with you; I am within you. Even in your darkness, I am here helping you in many ways. Stay with me here.*

Know that I am with you.

GENESIS 28:15

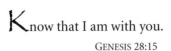

One of the hardest things about being sick is the big sense of aloneness I feel, my God. No matter how many people care about me, and help me, and reach out to me, I'm so aware of how alone I am here.

I know that we come into this world alone. And I know we come to our end here alone, even if we're surrounded by the people we love that we need to leave behind.

It's good to know that I can count on you being with me, through whatever I'm experiencing. So I won't be alone. Thank you for that, my God.

Job declared: "Even though God slays me, yet will I trust."

ADAPTED FROM JOB 13:15

—◄○►—

I am stunned by Job, O God of mystery. Struck low by the savage sufferings of life for no apparent reason, he still could trust you. I wish I could make his sentiments my own. I would like to be of such great faith in the midst of my anguish. Yet I know it would cost me much to make those words my own.

I would need to lose my distrust of you and believe in your providential care of my life. I would have to give up my need to know all the answers and keep control over every aspect of my life. I would have to give up trying to get you to always do things my way. I would need to accept paradox, ambiguity, and your love.

I am not that spiritually developed yet, mysterious God. When the sufferings of life seem to slay me, my trust wavers. When hard times come, I question whether you know what's happening. So my prayer is not only that you heal me but also that you help me come to trust you, whether you heal me or not.

Where are you, my God? And where am I? I don't even recognize myself anymore. My body is wasting away and is filled with pain. I don't feel like the self I've known. I feel lost and frightened.

Yet through all this suffering, I know you are with me. You know me and love me even when I hardly know myself. I count on you. Do not forsake me.

—◀o▶—

Blessed be the God and Father of our Lord Jesus Christ, the Father of mercies and the God of all consolation, who consoles us in all our affliction.

2 CORINTHIANS 1:3

My illness, saving God, leads me to be more solitary and focused on myself. I believe that's understandable. However, as I think of and pray for myself, help me feel a oneness with the vast number of other ill and wounded people all over the world. They are in hospitals, streets, and homes. Some are victims of accidents and battles.

At one time or another, we all suffer. I know it is part of our imperfect condition, and often an opportunity for growth in wisdom and compassion. May this time of suffering I share with many others be one of spiritual growth and courage—a time to recognize priorities—and a heartfelt turning to you. May it be an occasion that increases my compassion for others. Though we are miles apart, our hearts are very similar.

So, for myself and for the countless suffering people I do not know, I ask that you heal us, comfort us, and draw us closer together in our common adversity so that we may know we are never alone.

Wretched...
God, that's how I feel.

My body feels wretched beyond belief,
I'm aching and in pain.
I'm weak, without a trace of energy.
My spirit feels wretched;
my whole life feels wretched.

I'm not sure I can do this much longer.
I'm not even sure what the point of it all is.

And I don't feel the least bit like praying.

But, perhaps, the very fact
that I'm telling you all this is a prayer?

Into your hands I commit my spirit;
you will redeem me, Yahweh.

PSALM 31:5
Psalms Anew

O God,
your hands created and formed me
    and brought me to birth
as one you know through and through;
your hands have sheltered me
    and held me close
    through every step of my life;
and even now, in my sickness
and suffering,
your hands cradle me and bless me.

O God,
let me know that I need never fear,
I am in your hands
whether I ask to be there or not.
You will continue to hold me and be close
through all that is now and will be for me.

Some pray to you, attentive God, for a return to health. I cannot, for my illness is terminal. I will die in some weeks or months. For what, then, do I pray?

I pray that I may know you are at my side. You created me from nothing, and have guided me and loved me through all these years. Though no other person can accompany me as I pass from this world into eternity, you can, O God. I am never alone. May I become more aware of your presence.

I pray that you help ease my fears and strengthen my faith in you. My fears remind me of my weakness and sins; may my faith remind me of your love and forgiveness. My fears say my life will end; may my faith hint of the intense life you will give me. My fears say I will leave forever all those whom I love; may my faith tell my heart we will meet again with an even greater love.

I pray most of all in my final days that I may come to know you more, my God. Only in you will I find that for which I hunger. May I be able to make my own the words of your servant Augustine, who wrote so movingly, "Late have I loved you, O Beauty so ancient, O Beauty so new."

God, I feel scared.

I don't know what's going to become of me.
I try to do everything the doctor tells me,
everything that I know is good for me,
and I don't get any better.

I pray to you, I ask for your help,
I try to live my life like you would want,
but I don't get any better.

As the psalmist says,
"God, your thoughts are mysterious!
How vast is their sum."

I don't understand
why you don't answer my prayers.
So I pray with the psalmist,
"Close behind and close in front,
you hem me in,
shielding me with your hand."
Such knowledge is beyond
my understanding,
too high beyond my reach.

My God, maybe I don't have to understand,
but please increase my trust.

Now my soul is troubled. And what should I say—
'Father, save me from this hour'? No, it is for this
reason that I have come to this hour. Father, glorify
your name."

JOHN 12:27

—◄◦►—

If a seed placed in the ground could feel and think,
it would often find its "hour" bleak and unbear-
able. Down in the damp and darkness, pressures on
every side, no hint of the final blooming, it could
question its purpose. It could entertain thoughts of
giving up or ask to be saved from such earthbound
suffering. Yet some force of greater life urges it onward, upward, through dank soil into the air,
through nights and days, rain and sunlight, heat and
cold, until it thrills and glories in full bloom.

I have been created and placed in the ground of
this world. I often feel its pressures, darkness,
struggles, and sufferings, with no hint of a final
blooming. Yet I am urged onward, upward by the
call of the One who planted me. A high destiny
awaits me through and beyond all my obstacles. Shall
I say, "Save me from this hour?" No! It is for this
purpose—my eternal blooming and God's glory—
that I am here in this hour.

Breathe in me, O Spirit of God,
    and drive all evil away.
Renew my soul and heal my body,
    lift my heart this day.
Help me know how close you are
    and your great love for me.
Strengthen my faith that whatever comes
    I can say, "Let it be!"
For you love me so, that nothing occurs
    that lies beyond your will.
So take my chaos, pain, and doubt
    and bid my storms be still.
Calm my worries, weaken my fears,
    change my darkness to light.
For here I stand, the one you made,
    in whom you take delight.

Even though I walk in the dark valley,
I fear no evil;
for you are at my side.

PSALM 23:4
Psalms Anew

—◄o►—

When I struggle with pain that tortures me,
You walk with me, my God.
When my path is filled with worry and fear,
You walk with me, my God.
When sorrow and regret are haunting me,
You walk with me, my God.
When my life feels overwhelming
     and threatens to be too much,
You walk with me, my God.
When my time has come
     and death is waiting for me,
You walk with me, my God.
I count on you to be ever with me.
And so you are.

Elijah came to a broom tree in the desert. He sat under it and prayed that he might die. He said in his misery, "I have had enough, O God. Take my life."

ADAPTED FROM 1 KINGS 19:4

◄○►

Sometimes our pain and weakness seem more than we can bear. We struggle and work to keep them under control. We pray and hope that God will hear us and give us the relief that we so desperately crave. But our prayer seems unanswered. We don't think we can go on.

Sometimes we feel overwhelmed by depression. We sink into a place of helplessness and seeming despair. We don't want to fight anymore. We can't find the energy to make the effort.

Sometimes we simply give ourselves over into God's hands. We know our time is very short, and we say yes to our own experience.

In all these times, let us say, "I have had enough, O God. Take my life into your loving hands. I know you are with me and carry me through the difficult places."

That is why we never give up. Though our bodies are dying, our inner strength in the Lord is growing every day. These troubles and sufferings of ours are, after all, quite small and won't last very long. Yet this short time of distress will result in God's richest blessing upon us forever and ever! So we do not look at what we can see right now, the troubles all around us, but we look forward to the joys in heaven which we have not yet seen. The troubles will soon be over, but the joys to come will last forever.

2 CORINTHIANS 4:16–18

―◄○►―

This is the time, dear God of my life, to realize that your heart is truly my home, my refuge, my support. You are at my side, walking every step of the way with me. I couldn't get away from you if I tried.

I am the resurrection and the life. Those who believe in me, even though they die, will live....Do you
believe this?"

JOHN 11:25–26

◄○►

Terminal is the word I was told, gracious God. I will
die soon. Since my birth I have been on a journey
toward my death. I usually have kept myself from
realizing it because I want so much to live forever. I
cannot envision myself not existing.

Now I realize my fragile mortality more than I
ever have before. I am stunned to discover it, shocked
that it means me, not just other people. I feel angry,
insulted, sad, confused. I even question your goodness. Traces of doubt surface in my soul. I worry
about how much I will suffer before I die, and what
I will find after I die. Is what I have believed true?
Or are all my beliefs wishful thinking?

Through the Scriptures you ask me, "Do you
believe this?" Do I believe with conviction that you
live and that I will live, too? Though my faith is far
from strong, I honestly say, "I do!" Like the unnamed
man in the gospels, I say, "I do believe, help my un-
belief!" I entrust myself to you, sinful though I am.
Take my hand, O Christ, and when the day of my
death arrives, lead me into that true, intense life that
is not terminal, that is your life—and mine!

Cast your cares on God,
   who will sustain you.

PSALM 55:22

Gracious God, sometimes I feel
   so overwhelmed with my life.
It all feels like such a burden,
   and I'm not sure I can handle it.
I don't know what's going to become of me.
I am sick, weak, and scared so much of the time,
   and I feel helpless to change things.

Help me to take you at your word.
Help me to "cast my cares" on you and trust
   that you will support and sustain me.

—◦—

In your mind's eye, picture yourself burdened with
all your distress—bent over with a load of weari-
ness and sickness and pain on your back. See your
slow and faltering steps as you make your way toward God, who is waiting for you with open arms.

As God reaches out to you, unload your burden
into those loving arms. Watch as God sets your heavy
load aside and reaches again toward you. With trust
and love, walk into those arms that are waiting for
you—always warm and always open. God has promised to be always with you, and will give you strength
and hold you close on your journey.

When my pain grows and I struggle
    with its intensity,
God, remind me you are near.
Hold me in your hands.

When I fear dying,
    yet cannot go on as I am,
God, remind me you are near.
Hold me in your hands.

When no one seems to understand my cries,
God, remind me you are near.
Hold me in your hands.

When I wonder why this is
    happening to me,
God, remind me you are near.
Hold me in your hands.

When even my life seems to fail me,
God, remind me you are near.
Hold me in your hands.

My God, my God,
why have you deserted me?
Far from my prayer, from the words I cry?
I call all day, my God,
but you never answer;
all night long I call and cannot rest.

. . . .

Do not stand aside, Yahweh.
O my strength, come quickly to my help.

PSALM 22:1–2,19
Psalms Anew

◄○►

All adventures, especially into new territory, are
scary, for I've never been there before. Whether the
road leads into love, pain, illness, an operation, in-
capacitation, inner turmoil, or eternity, fear is my
companion.

But so are you, my God.

May I hold your hand?

I cried, fearful of what was happening
    to me,
stunned by the suffering and a strange
    vulnerability.
If only someone would save me from this!
But it continued, and I was born
    into the world.
Thus, the process of birth.

I cried, afraid of separating and leaving.
I felt alone and had a strong longing to stay.
If only someone would tell me
    I didn't have to go!
But insistence prevailed,
    and I went off to school.
Thus, the process of learning.

I cried many times when life was difficult
    and painful.
At times, I felt helpless, confused,
    and angered.
I looked for someone to make it easier
    and save me.
But life went on and I matured.
Thus, the process of growth.

I cried, saddened by my weakness
    and illness.
I wept to think of losing life, strength,
    and the ones I love.
I prayed, asking God to save me from this.
But it continued, and I left this world.
Thus, the process of death.

I laughed, danced, sang,
    and felt an overflowing, ecstatic joy.
I had never experienced the thrill
    of such happiness before.
I looked for someone with whom
    to share such a life,
    and God was there, and others I loved.
Thus, ended the process of becoming whole.

Gracious God, I am ill and fearful of death. Like a child asking to have a wonderful story retold, tell me once again what will happen to all your faithful people who die.

—◄o►—

So it is with the resurrection of the dead. What is sown is perishable, what is raised is imperishable. It is sown in dishonor, it is raised in glory. It is sown in weakness, it is raised in power. It is sown a physical body, it is raised a spiritual body.

1 CORINTHIANS 15:42–44

They will hunger no more
        and thirst no more;
    the sun will not strike them,
        nor any scorching heat;

. . . .

and God will wipe away
    every tear from their eyes.

REVELATION 7:16–17

"What no eye has seen, nor ear heard,
    nor the human heart conceived,
what God has prepared for those
    who love him."

1 CORINTHIANS 2:9

When from our exile
God leads us home again
we'll think we're dreaming.
We shall be singing,
laughing for happiness,
we'll think we're dreaming!

People will say
"Their God does wonders!"
Yes, you do wonders,
God ever with us.

You bring us to life
like flowers in the desert bloom
when new rain comes.

We sow life in tears,
but you make our harvest
more than we hoped for!

When you lead us home
and love us completely,
we'll think we're dreaming!

Acknowledgments

Every effort has been made to locate and secure permission for the inclusion of all copyrighted material in this book. If any such acknowledgments have been inadvertently omitted, the publisher would appreciate receiving full information so that proper credit may be given in future editions.

The psalms in this book are from *Psalms Anew: In Inclusive Language,* compiled by Nancy Schreck and Maureen Leach (Winona, Minn.: Saint Mary's Press, 1986). Copyright © 1986 by Saint Mary's Press. All rights reserved.

The scriptural quotations cited as "adapted from" are freely adapted and are not to be interpreted or used as official translations of the Scriptures.

The scriptural quotations in this book, except where noted, are from the *New Revised Standard Version of the Bible*, copyright © 1989 by the Division of Christian Education of the National Council of the Churches of Christ in the United States of America. All rights reserved.

The quotation on page 7 is from *Suffering* by Louis Evely (New York: Herder and Herder, 1967), pages 148—149. Copyright © 1967 by Herder and Herder.

The quotation on page 13 is used only in part from pages 2 and 3 of *Shadowlands* by William Nicholson, copyright © 1990 by William Nicholson. Used by permission of Dulton Signet, a division of Penguin Books (USA) Inc.

The quotation on page 51 is from *Wheels in the Air,* by William T. Joyner (Philadelphia: Pilgrim Press, 1968), page 63. Copyright © 1968 by United Church Press.

Other Books
by Joan Guntzelman

Blessing Life's Losses
Letting Go and Moving On

"*Blessing Life's Losses* could only have been written by someone who has been there— deeply, prayerfully, and with immense awareness." —Richard Rohr, OFM, Center for Action and Contemplation, Albuquerque, New Mexico

The sixteen reflections in this book assist readers in grieving life's losses due to aging, broken relationships, destroyed self-respect, the death of companion animals, the death of loved ones, and so on. Each reflection begins with an evocative story, includes a brief commentary, and then invites reflection through a variety of exercises.

124 Prayers for Caregivers

"Sensitive not only to the varying intensity of prayer, but also to the multiplicity of its presentations, these succinct pages of commentary, wisdom, and meditation offer perspective as well as faith and credible hope. A manual for every human being who has occasion either to give or—perhaps more unusually—to have to receive help." —*Publishers Weekly*

The 124 prayers in this book offer a powerful source of strength and consolation. Each prayer includes a brief quotation from the Bible or another source, several lines of reflection, and a closing petition. While praying, we remind ourselves that God stands with us in our caregiving. In rewarding times, when everything goes well and we feel full of light and blessing, and in dark times, when things are especially difficult, we remind ourselves that God is never absent.